Make
every day
count

Heartfelt

Heartfelt